11/16/16

The Causes of the
American Revolution

John Perritano

CRABTREE
Publishing Company
www.crabtreebooks.com

Understanding The American Revolution

Author: John Perritano
Publishing plan research and development:
Sean Charlebois, Reagan Miller
Crabtree Publishing Company
Editors: Leslie Jenkins, Janet Sweet, Lynn Peppas
Proofreaders: Lisa Slone, Kelly McNiven
Editorial director: Kathy Middleton
Production coordinator: Shivi Sharma
Creative director: Amir Abbasi
Cover design: Samara Parent, Margaret Amy Salter
Photo research: Nivisha Sinha
Maps: Paul Brinkdopke
Production coordinator and prepress technician: Samara Parent
Print coordinator: Katherine Berti

Written, developed, and produced by Planman Technologies

Cover: From the left, Benjamin Franklin, John Adams, and Thomas Jefferson. Franklin and Adams help revise the Declaration of Independence.

Title page: (Main) Minutemen confront British forces.
(Bottom) Two soldiers in the Continental Army march through the snow playing a fife and drum.

Photographs and Reproductions
Front cover: Shutterstock; Title Page: Library of congress; Library of congress;Table of Content: Architect of the Capitol; Library of congress; Library of congress; Library of congress; Usawicka / Shutterstock; Architect of the Capitol; Introduction: Library of congress; Chapter 1: Library of congress; Chapter 2: Library of congress; Chapter 3: Library of congress; Chapter 4: Library of congress; Chapter 5: Library of congress; Page 5: Architect of the Capitol; Page 9: ©B Christopher / Alamy / IndiaPicture; Page 10: Universal / IndiaPicture; Page 11: Library of congress; Page 12: Mary / IndiaPicture; Page 13: Library of congress; Page 15: Library of congress; Page 16: Everett / IndiaPicture; Page 17: Library of congress; Page 18: ©The Art Archive / Alamy / IndiaPicture; Page 19: Getty Images; Page 21: ©Stock Montage, Inc. / Alamy / IndiaPicture; Page 22: Library of congress; Page 23: Library of congress; Page 24: ©Alan King engraving / Alamy / IndiaPicture; Page 25: Library of congress; Page 26: Library of congress; Page 27: Library of congress; Page 28: Library of congress; Page 29: Universal / IndiaPicture; Page 30: Usawicka / Shutterstock; Page 31: ©Peter Vallance / Alamy / IndiaPicture; Page 32: Library of congress; Page 33: Library of congress; Page 35: Library of congress; Page 36: Library of congress; Page 37: Library of congress; Page 38: Library of congress; Page 39: Library of congress (t); Library of congress (bl); Library of congress (br); Page 40: Library of congress; Page 41: Architect of the Capitol; (t = top, b = bottom, l = left, c = center, r = right, bl = bottom left, br = bottom right, bkgd = background, fgd = foreground)

Library and Archives Canada Cataloguing in Publication

Perritano, John
      The causes of the American Revolution / John Perritano.

(Understanding the American Revolution)
Includes bibliographical references and index.
Issued also in electronic format.
ISBN 978-0-7787-0804-9 (bound).--ISBN 978-0-7787-0815-5 (pbk.)

      1. United States--History--Revolution, 1775-1783--Causes--Juvenile literature. 2. United States--Politics and government--To 1775--Juvenile literature. 3. Great Britain--Politics and government--1760-1789--Juvenile literature. I. Title. II. Series: Understanding the American Revolution (St. Catharines, Ont.)

E210.P467 2013   j973.3'11   C2013-900232-4

Library of Congress Cataloging-in-Publication Data

CIP available at Library of Congress

Crabtree Publishing Company

Printed in Canada/022013/BF20130114

www.crabtreebooks.com   1-800-387-7650

Published in Canada
Crabtree Publishing
616 Welland Ave.
St. Catharines, Ontario
L2M 5V6

Published in the United States
Crabtree Publishing
PMB 59051
350 Fifth Avenue, 59th Floor
New York, New York 10118

Published in the United Kingdom
Crabtree Publishing
Maritime House
Basin Road North, Hove
BN41 1WR

Published in Australia
Crabtree Publishing
3 Charles Street
Coburg North
VIC 3058

TABLE *of* CONTENTS

Introduction

The American Revolution began as a fight for colonists' **rights**. The fight exploded into an all-out war and ended with the creation of the United States of America.

Major Events

1775

April 19
Battles of Lexington and Concord

May 10
Americans capture Fort Ticonderoga

June 17
British losses near Bunker Hill

July 2
George Washington takes command of Continental Army

Liberty or Death

As dawn broke on April 19, 1775, British soldiers faced a group of armed Americans in Lexington, Massachusetts. "Disperse you villains, you rebels! . . . Lay down your arms!" the British commander ordered. A shot rang out—the first of the American Revolutionary War. The British **surrendered** six years later.

The War Begins

No one knows who fired the first shot of the war. Yet, one thing was certain—independence from Great Britain was not the plan of Americans in April 1775. In many ways, however, independence was to be expected. The relationship between Great Britain and its 13 **American colonies** had grown more and more tense. By 1775, it seemed war was the only way to solve their differences.

The battles at Lexington and nearby Concord unleashed outrage across the colonies. Virginian Patrick Henry summed up the feelings of many Americans when he declared, "I know not what course others may take, but as for me, give me liberty or give me death."

> *What a glorious morning this is!*
>
> —**Patriot** leader Samuel Adams after the Battle of Lexington, April 1775

War Cry

The British thought they could easily crush the rebellion. They were, after all, the strongest army in the world. However, what the Americans lacked in military skill they made up for in determination and courage.

The Americans won two victories in the summer of 1775. The following March, the British army and their supporters left Boston for good. Still, each victory seemed to teeter on the edge of defeat. **Patriot** soldiers did not have enough guns, ammunition, or blankets. They were hungry and worn out. Yet, the **bedraggled** Americans rallied every time they seemed about to fall.

Wanted: Allies

By July 1776, the colonies decided to declare independence. But freedom was hard to imagine without a military victory. The Americans needed help, so Benjamin Franklin and others traveled to Europe to find **allies**. In 1777, the Continental Army soundly defeated the British at Saratoga, New York. Once the Patriots had proved they could fight the British, the French entered the war.

Southern Strategy

The British shifted their military **strategy** after Saratoga. For years, they tried to cut off New England from the rest of the colonies. When this proved impossible, they marched south. This decision stretched supplies too thin. The British surrendered on October 19, 1781, at Yorktown, Virginia, effectively ending the war. The United States emerged a free nation.

People in the War

Benjamin Franklin

Benjamin Franklin was born on January 17, 1706. He led a busy life, being a printer, diplomat, inventor, educator, and scientist. He invented the lightning rod, the Franklin stove, and bifocals, and organized the first public library. After helping to write the Declaration of Independence, Franklin convinced France to help the United States in their struggle for independence. Franklin also became one of the framers of the Constitution. He died on April 17, 1790.

Surrender at Yorktown

Hudson's Bay Company

Nova Scotia

Province of Quebec

Massachusetts

claimed by New York and New Hampshire

New Hampshire

Boston

New York

Massachusetts

Rhode Island
Connecticut

Pennsylvania

New York

New Jersey

Philadelphia

Delaware

Baltimore

Maryland

Virginia

Indian Reserve

Spanish Louisiana

North Carolina

South Carolina

Georgia

Charleston

ATLANTIC OCEAN

West Florida

East Florida

Gulf of Mexico

	British Territory
	Thirteen Colonies (British)
	Spanish Territory
●	major city
– –	Proclamation Line of 1763*

0   125   250 miles
0   125   250 kilometers

*This line shows the farthest west British settlers were allowed to go. The rest of the land was reserved for Native Americans.

North America before the American Revolution

Hudson's Bay Company

claimed by New York
and New Hampshire

claimed by New York
and Massachusetts

Massachusetts

New York

New Hampshire

Boston

Massachusetts

Rhode Island
Connecticut

Pennsylvania

New York

New Jersey

Philadelphia

Spanish
Louisiana

Baltimore

Delaware

Maryland

Virginia

claimed by
Virginia

**North
Carolina**

claimed by
North Carolina

**ATLANTIC
OCEAN**

claimed by
South Carolina

**South
Carolina**

claimed by Georgia

Georgia

Charleston

claimed by
United States
and Spain

0   125   250 miles
0   125   250 kilometers

Gulf of Mexico

Spanish
Florida

Legend	
	British Territory
	United States
	Spanish Territory
	territory claimed by two states
	territory claimed by U.S. and Spain
●	major city

The United States of America in 1783

French and Indian War

Christopher Columbus landed in the Americas by mistake in 1492. His arrival sparked a mad dash to control the New World. Wars, such as the French and Indian War, were fought over territory. The cost of this war in turn helped spark the American Revolution.

⤳ What Do You Know!

VIKINGS IN THE NEW WORLD

Christopher Columbus is no longer thought to have been the first European in America. In about 970 A.D., a Norwegian sailor, Bjarni Herjulfsson, saw an unknown shore after being blown off course to Greenland. Thirty years later, Leif Ericson, came back to explore. Ericson and his crew are thought to have explored Canada's Atlantic coast and possibly as far south as Virginia. They tried to build settlements but they did not succeed.

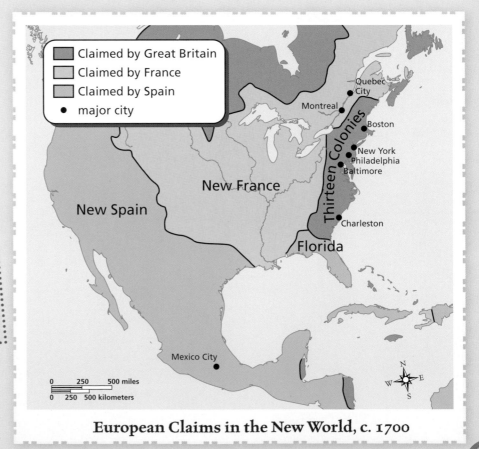

Claimed by Great Britain
Claimed by France
Claimed by Spain
• major city

Quebec City
Montreal
Boston
New York
Philadelphia
Baltimore
Thirteen Colonies
New France
New Spain
Charleston
Florida
Mexico City

0   250   500 miles
0   250   500 kilometers

N W E S

European Claims in the New World, c. 1700

New World Rising

The superpowers of Europe eyed the Americas for its vast resources. Europeans thought the gold, silver, and other treasures were theirs for the taking. British and French settlers **colonized** large portions of North America. The French settled in Canada, Louisiana, and elsewhere. The British colonized New England, Virginia, and other areas. Both nations competed for furs, tobacco, and other trade goods. By early 1754, the French occupied the Ohio River Valley. The British were upset. They had claimed that territory for themselves. They asked the French to leave, but France refused.

Virginia's colonial governor Robert Dinwiddie ordered a military outpost built in the region. Dinwiddie sent a small group of **militia** commanded by Colonel George Washington to help. The French forced the British out before the fortress was finished and before Washington arrived. The French then built Fort Duquesne in its place. Located in what is today Pittsburgh, Pennsylvania, Fort Duquesne was a constant reminder of French power in the region. Washington ended up building a small outpost east of Fort Duquesne. Its name was Fort Necessity.

A small French force scouted Fort Necessity on May 28, 1754. The two armies clashed. The French retreated. A few weeks later, a much larger French force surrounded the fort and forced Washington to surrender.

Major Events

1754
May 28
French and British clash at Fort Necessity; French and Indian War (Seven Years' War) begins

1759
British troops capture Quebec City

1760
British troops capture Montreal

1763
French and Indian War ends
May
Pontiac's Rebellion

1764
Sugar Act passed

George Washington in Virginia militia uniform

Seven Years of War

The fighting in the Ohio River Valley quickly spread into a major conflict between France and England. The war engulfed Europe, India, and the Caribbean. Known as the Seven Years' War, the fighting that took place in North America was called the French and Indian War (1754–1763). The clash in North America not only involved the British and the French, but their Native American allies too.

French Domination

The French dominated the battlefield for the first three years of the war. British fortunes changed by 1758. A year later, British troops swept into Canada and captured what is today Quebec City. Montreal fell the following year.

The British defeated the French, capturing Canada and all French territory east of the Mississippi River. Oddly enough, the victory also marked the beginning of the end of Britain's domination over America.

Who Pays?

The French defeat expanded Britain's territory in America, but it came with a heavy price. Nine years of fighting left the British with a debt of nearly £130 million (about $12 billion in today's dollars). Such an enormous debt was hurting the British **economy**. Moreover, the government now had to feed, clothe, and pay 20,000 soldiers to guard all this new territory.

Someone had to pay the bill—but who? The obvious answer was to increase **taxes** on people in Britain. However, raising taxes at home was unpopular. The nation was already financially strained. So King George III and **Parliament** decided the Americans should pay down the war debt themselves. They also said the colonies should pay for their own protection.

People in the War

King George III

King George III reigned over the British Empire at the time of the American Revolution. He was born in 1738 and became king in 1760. He was king during a time of struggle between Britain and France for dominance in Europe and the Americas. While his reign saw the loss of the American colonies, he also ruled over the defeat of Napoleon in 1815. He died five years later in 1820.

Trouble on the Frontier

Guarding the frontier had become a major headache for the British. The British gave their Native American allies lavish gifts during the war in exchange for their help. But the blankets, trinkets, and tools stopped coming when the fighting ended. The Native Americans were angry.

The Native Americans were also troubled that their home in the Ohio River Valley was now being settled by colonists. Americans rushed to build farms, homes, and roads. By May 1763, the Native Americans had had enough. They rose up in a rebellion. Led by Ottawa Chief Pontiac, the tribes destroyed frontier settlements. They captured British military outposts and they killed American settlers.

This uprising—called Pontiac's Rebellion—forced the British to clamp down on American westward expansion. King George III and Parliament drew up the Proclamation of 1763. This measure stopped the colonists from settling west of the Appalachian Mountains. The Proclamation also recognized each Native American group as an independent nation.

The proclamation kept out the colonial farmers who saw their fortunes in the western lands. It also stirred up fears that the king was limiting colonists' rights. The British put troops along the Appalachian boundary. Many colonists feared the king would use those soldiers to enforce unjust laws.

Major Campbell arguing with Pontiac

> *. . . [F]rom and after the twenty ninth day of September [1764] . . . there shall be raised, levied, collected, and paid, unto his Majesty . . . for and upon all white or clayed sugars . . . ; for and upon indigo, and coffee of foreign produce or manufacture; for an upon all wines (except French wine;) . . . for and upon all foreign linen cloth called Cambrick and French Lawns . . . the several rates and duties following. . .*
>
> —excerpt from the Sugar Act, 1764

The Sugar Act

Ruling a colony across an ocean was a tricky business. The distance and lack of communication let British officials ignore the needs of the colonies. British leaders often called the colonists "children" who had to be watched over and, if necessary, made to obey. In their view, the American colonists had to abide by any decision handed down by the king and Parliament.

To help fill the treasury, Britain's prime minister George Grenville proposed a series of laws to **levy** taxes on the colonies. The British were upset that American merchants avoided paying taxes on molasses. Often, molasses was illegally **smuggled** from the French and Spanish West Indies. Molasses, which is made from boiled sugar, is the main ingredient of rum, a popular alcoholic drink.

Prime Minister George Grenville

MOLASSES, SUGAR, AND SLAVERY

The Caribbean islands produced large amounts of sugar, molasses, and rum during the colonial era. Sugar cane is grown in warm climates. During colonial times, enslaved people from Africa harvested the sugar cane and milled sugar from the cane. Some juice was squeezed from the sugar cane, and this was boiled into molasses. Molasses was often used to make rum. In the colonial Caribbean and some southern colonies, most of the sugar processing was done with slave labor.

Seeds of Discontent

In 1733 Parliament had passed the Molasses Act. The act placed a six-cent tax on each gallon of molasses imported into the colonies. Parliament replaced the Molasses Act with the Sugar Act in 1764. The new law reduced the tax on molasses to three cents per gallon. However, it called for stricter enforcement of smuggling laws. The Sugar Act also levied new taxes on Madeira wine from Portugal and added other **duties** to regulate trade. Grenville did not think his proposal would anger the Americans. Only smugglers had to worry, he said.

Grenville was wrong about the American reaction. Like Great Britain, the colonies were struggling. Colonists could not afford any new taxes. Even the king's colonial representatives were upset. Massachusetts's governor Francis Bernard said American businessmen could not afford even a small tax on sugar.

Boston beer maker Samuel Adams was one of the first to criticize the new policy. He predicted the Sugar Act was the first step on the road to **tyranny**. "For if our trade may be taxed, why not our lands?" Adams asked. "Why not the produce of our lands, and in short, everything we possess or make use of?"

The seeds of **discontent** were taking root.

Colonists protesting British taxes

What Do You Think?

Should Britain have expected the Americans to pay for their own defense? Why or why not?

The Screws Tighten

J ames Otis found his voice. Once a loyal British subject, the Boston lawyer was now questioning Britain's colonial policies. "Taxation without representation," he said, was wrong. The phrase "no taxation without representation" soon became the rallying cry that united the colonies.

Major Events

1764

April 5
Parliament agrees to Sugar Act

September 1
Parliament passes **Currency** Act

1765

February 17
Parliament passes Stamp Act

March 24
Quartering Act passes

Parliamentary Acts Taxing the Colonies		
Act	*Year*	*Purpose*
Sugar Act	1764	tax on sugar and molasses; replaced Molasses Act of 1733
Currency Act	1764	took paper bills out of circulation; hard coins became the only legal currency
Stamp Act	1765	tax on paper; taxed almanacs, cards, commercial papers, dice, legal documents, newspapers, and pamphlets
Quartering Act	1765	colonists to provide housing and amenities for British soldiers
Townshend Acts	1767	taxes on glass, lead, paint, paper, and tea
'Intolerable' Acts	1774	closed Boston **Harbor**; put in military government in Mass.; protected British officials who had committed crimes; gave lots of land to Quebec

> " *. . . The General Assembly of this Colony have the only and sole exclusive Right and Power to lay Taxes and Impositions upon the Inhabitants of this Colony . . .* "
>
> —from Virginia Resolves, a series of resolutions passed by the Virginia House of Burgesses in response to the Stamp Act of 1765

Bitter Reaction

The Sugar Act had hit a nerve. Several colonial **legislatures** tried to resist the law. Each claimed the British government had no right to **impose** taxes on Americans. Local merchants in American ports made it difficult for the Royal Navy to stop smugglers. Although many colonists felt the tax was unjust, it had little impact on most because the law did not directly affect them.

Also in 1764, Parliament passed the Currency Act. This law banned the colonies from using the paper money used since the French and Indian War. Parliament approved the measure because British merchants did not trust the value of colonial "bills of credit." They wanted to be paid in British currency. Parliament also hoped the law would reduce Great Britain's debt.

A 1700s cartoon showing American colonists begging for the repeal of the taxes, while tax officials sit comfortably with their gains.

Stamping Out the Debt

Back in Great Britain, Grenville wanted to impose more new taxes on the colonies in 1765. He brushed aside the worries of the colonists. Grenville's lack of concern could be felt across the Atlantic. As prime minister, Grenville was not a popular Royal official. He did not express himself well and he lacked imagination. He was also power hungry and determined to control all the appointments to the king's government.

While the Sugar and Currency Acts did not make the average colonist angry, many Americans were very upset at the Stamp Act. This new law taxed anything requiring the use of paper, including court documents, newspapers, playing cards, and property deeds. Colonists had to buy the stamps if they wanted their business to be legal. A person could not transfer property, write a will, or mail a letter without a Royal stamp. The stamps forced nearly every American to pay more for the things they used every day.

What Do You Think?

Why do you think the Stamp Act made people more upset than the other taxes?

Stamps like these were attached to documents to show the Stamp Act tax had been paid.

Patrick Henry in the House of Burgesses

The Colonists' Reaction

Americans first reacted calmly when rumors of the Stamp Act filtered back to them. But by June 1765, the colonists had learned about all the terms. Their response was swift and harsh. Colonial legislatures formally protested the measure. The loudest cry came from Virginia, where the House of Burgesses declared that only colonial assemblies had the "sole right to lay taxes" on the people they represented.

Patrick Henry, the newest member of the House, was the most vocal. He introduced a series of resolutions called the Virginia Resolves. A resolve is a formal expression of an opinion. One resolve read: ". . . the inhabitants of this Colony, are not bound to yield obedience to any law or ordinance whatever, designed to impose any taxation whatsoever upon them, other than the laws or ordinances of the General Assembly . . ."

The burgesses never agreed to this, or a second more harshly-worded resolve. Still, both were printed in newspapers across the colonies, fanning the flames of dissent.

What Do You Know!

HOUSE OF BURGESSES

The Virginia House of Burgesses was an assembly of representatives from all of Virginia's settlements, like today's state legislature. It was the first of these in the British Empire outside of Great Britain. It was established in 1619 and was a major part of Virginia's government until the Revolutionary War.

PROTESTS While the politicians talked, others took to the streets, chanting "no taxation without representation." **Radical** groups, or groups with extreme opinions and actions against taxation, formed. The first appeared in Boston. They called themselves the Loyal Nine. Made up of local merchants and craftsmen, the Loyal Nine's leader was local brewer Samuel Adams.

Educated at Harvard, Adams had little interest in running a brewery. He loved politics instead. Adams and his group organized demonstrations directing their rage at the stamp officials.

> *How easy it is for some . . . wicked men . . . to raise suspicions and jealousies in the minds of the populace and enrage them against the innocent.*
>
> —Thomas Hutchinson, 1765

ATTACKS On August 14, 1765, a Boston mob marched to the city's wharf and destroyed the building where they believed the stamps were to be kept. They then went to the home of Andrew Oliver, the stamp distributor in Boston. The mob shattered windows and ransacked his house. Oliver quickly quit his job. The mob continued their destructive ways. On August 26, angry demonstrators destroyed the house of Thomas Hutchinson, the lieutenant governor of Massachusetts. Bostonians believed he supported the Stamp Act. Hutchinson's family ran for their lives. The following day, Hutchinson voiced his opposition to the act.

The Stamp Act riots

HUTCHINSON'S ACCOUNT Thomas Hutchinson was a target of the colonists, who believed he supported the Stamp Act. He wrote this first-hand account of what happened to himself and Andrew Oliver.

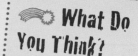
"The mob followed down King Street to Oliver's dock, near which Mr. Oliver had lately erected a building, which, it was conjectured, he designed for a stamp office. This was laid flat to the ground in a few minutes. From thence the mob proceeded for Fort Hill, but Mr. Oliver's house being in the way, they endeavored to force themselves into it, and being opposed, broke the windows, beat down the doors, entered, and destroyed part of his furniture, and continued in riot until midnight, before they separated. . . . Mr. Oliver came to a sudden resolution to resign his office before another night.

"The next evening, the mob surrounded the house of the lieutenant-governor and chief justice [Hutchinson]. He was at Mr. Oliver's house when it was assaulted. . . . A report was soon spread, that he was a favourer of the stamp act, and had encouraged it by letters to the ministry. Upon notice of the approach of the people, he caused the doors and windows to be barred; and remained in the house. The doors were immediately split to pieces with broad axes, and a way made there, and at the windows, for the entry of the mob; which poured in, and filled, in an instant, every room in the house.

"The lieutenant-governor . . . directed his children, and the rest of his family, to leave the house immediately, determining to keep possession himself. His eldest daughter, after going a little way from the house, returned, and refused to quit it, unless her father would do the like. This caused him to depart from his resolutions, a few minutes before the mob entered. . . ."

Thomas Hutchinson

The Flame Spreads

Boston was not the only colonial city full of anger in 1765. Riots had broken out across the colonies by the end of the summer. Radical groups formed in almost every major city. They bullied stamp officers into resigning their posts. Mobs destroyed the stamps before they were unloaded from British ships. Things were so bad that, by November, almost no one would dare work as a Royal stamp distributor. As the riots continued, merchants decided to **boycott** British businesses, hoping to make the British economy suffer.

The Stamp Congress

On October 7, 1765, representatives from nine colonies met in New York City to discuss the crisis. One speaker, Christopher Gadsden from South Carolina, said the colonies should not act individually. Instead, all 13 colonies should speak in one voice. "There ought to be no New England man, no New Yorker, known on the continent, but all of us."

Unity among the 13 colonies was a novel concept and one that would be tested in years to come. The delegates agreed to write a Declaration of Rights to present to King George. In this declaration, the colonists said that England did not have the authority to tax the colonies without their consent. No one knew whether the king would listen.

> "
> . . .[A]ll will be over with the whole. There ought to be no New-England man, no New-Yorker, known on the Continent; but all of us Americans.
>
> —Christopher Gadsen, 1765
> "

Quartering Act

The colonists soon had another cause to be angry. Each year the cost of housing and feeding the king's soldiers in America increased. In order to pay for this, Parliament passed the Quartering Act in March 1765. It forced the colonies to provide housing for British troops. The law also required the colonies to give the troops supplies, such as firewood, candles, and cider or beer.

As violence over the Stamp Act grew, soldiers marched east to be closer to the larger cities. Most colonists had a fear of standing armies. They would rather have local militias that could be called to duty during a crisis and later disbanded. The colonists also believed the cost of housing British troops was an illegal tax. The colonists feared King George III would use his troops to crush **dissent** over his unpopular policies.

The Quartering Act required colonists to house soldiers. If colonists did not have a barn or other building, the soldiers would share the family's home.

Repeal

By the time news of the Stamp Act crisis reached Britain, King George had dismissed Grenville and replaced him with a new prime minister, Charles Watson-Wentworth, Marquess of Rockingham. Rockingham did not support the Stamp Act. He urged its repeal when London's merchants complained t he American boycott was hurting their businesses.

Parliament went along with the prime minister's suggestion— but only under one condition. Parliament wanted to send a clear message to the colonists that it and the king were still in charge. To that end, Parliament passed the Declaratory Act. The act decreed that the colonies "have been, are, and of right, ought to be subordinate unto, and dependent upon the imperial crown and parliament of Great Britain," meaning that the colonies had to obey the king and Parliament. King George approved the Stamp Act's repeal and the Declaratory Act on March 18.

Weeks later, news of the Stamp Act's repeal reached America. People took to the streets in celebration. Fireworks colored the skies above Boston. John Hancock, a local merchant, "treated the populace with a Pipe of Madeira Wine." The colonial legislatures, except Virginia's, sent the king proclamations of thanks.

What Do You Know!

Why do you think Parliament wanted to say they were in charge in the Declaratory Act?

An artist drew this cartoon about the repeal of the Stamp Act. In the cartoon, officials are saying a funeral mass for the Stamp Act or perhaps for Britain's future in America.

The Sons of Liberty

A group of shopkeepers, craftsmen, and merchants took a more violent stance as the debate over the Stamp Act lingered. They organized themselves into a radical group. Its first name was the Loyal Nine. In time, they became the Sons of Liberty.

The Sons of Liberty used intimidation against the British. They met in secret to plan their activities. Once they hung an **effigy** of Andrew Oliver, the distributor of stamps in Massachusetts, from a tree on Newbury Street in Boston. When British officials ordered the local sheriffs to remove the display, they refused. The lawmen feared for their lives.

By the end of 1765, the Sons of Liberty were in every colony. They forced stamp distributors to resign. They pressured shopkeepers not to import British goods. By early 1766, the Sons of Liberty had forced many Royal officials into hiding. The group eventually outnumbered British troops in the colonies. The ranks of the Sons of Liberty became larger and more powerful as the crisis with Britain grew.

> *The Sons of Liberty on the 14th of August 1765, a Day which ought to be forever remembered in America, animated with a **zeal** for their country then upon the brink of destruction, and resolved, at once to save her. . . .*
>
> —from a 1765 *Boston Gazette* article written by Samuel Adams, referring to the anti-Stamp Act activists for the first time in print as "Sons of Liberty"

The Sons of Liberty are remembered for **tarring and feathering** Royal officials.

The Party is Over

Joy over the Stamp Act's repeal was short-lived. The idea of forcing Americans to pay down Britain's debt and pay for their own defense had not gone away. Instead, it took on another form. This time it came from Charles Townshend, chancellor of the Exchequer. The Exchequer is the name of the British treasury.

Townshend proposed a series of tax measures in May 1767. It was called the Revenue Act. It was also known as the Townshend Acts, or the Townshend Duties. The law forced Americans to pay a duty on imported products from Britain, including lead, glass, paint, paper, wine, and tea.

People in the War

Charles Townshend

Charles Townshend was born into a minor noble family in 1725. He served in several government positions before becoming chancellor of the Exchequer. The Exchequer is an **archaic** name for the treasury. The chancellor of the Exchequer was responsible for all of the government's money. Townshend died in 1767 before the taxation conflicts with the colonies broke down into war.

Charles Townshend

Constitutional Rights

The American response was quick and predictable. On December 30, 1767, the Massachusetts House of Representatives wrote a letter that it planned to send to every colony. The Revenue Act, the letter said, was an infringement upon the colonies' "natural and Constitutional rights."

The Crown ordered Massachusetts to **rescind**, or take back, the letter. If not, Governor Francis Bernard threatened to shut down the assembly. Prompted by Samuel Adams and James Otis, the House stood its ground. When Bernard got word of the House's decision, he screamed, "Samuel Adams! Every dip of his pen stings like a horned snake." Bernard dissolved the legislature.

John Dickinson

3

The Boston Massacre

Major Events

1767

June 29
Townshend
Revenue Act passes

1768

October 1
British troops
occupy Boston

1770

March 5
Boston Massacre

Rage against the British grew in every city and colony. However, it boiled over into bloodshed in the city of Boston.

The Lobsterbacks

John Hancock was as good a smuggler as anyone in America. Smuggling was a respectable way to make a living. To cut down on the illegal trade, the Townshend Acts gave British officials the right to search an individual's property for smuggled **commodities** such as molasses, tea, and wine.

Armed with the new law, the Crown took aim against Hancock. In May 1768, one of Hancock's ships arrived in Boston Harbor. Its name was the *Liberty*, and its cargo hold was crammed with smuggled wine.

Ships in Boston Harbor were a cause of conflict leading up to the Revolutionary War. Some ships were even targeted by Patriot radicals during the Boston Tea Party, shown here.

The harbor official who inspected the ship complained that its captain had threatened him after suspecting the ship carried illegal cargo. Customs agents seized the *Liberty*. A crowd flew into a rage when they saw officials **confiscating** Hancock's property. The mob attacked the customs agents with clubs. The agents fled to a British warship in the harbor. The crowd then set fires all along Boston's wharf.

Violence in Boston was out of control. Governor Bernard asked that British soldiers occupy the city. By fall, British **regulars** marched down Boston's streets. The Americans called the soldiers "lobsterbacks." Their bright red uniforms were a scary sight.

> *I will never think of repealing it, until I see America prostrate at my feet.*
>
> —Lord Frederick North, British statesman and chancellor of the Exchequer, speaking about the Revenue Act 1767

Boycott, Again

Colonial merchants hoped to end the Townshend Acts by again boycotting British-made goods. Southern farmers refused to import slaves from British traders. Women stopped serving British tea. Girls and their mothers made dresses with "homespun" American cloth instead of British fabric. Britain's leaders would not relent. They kept the duties in place.

British soldiers in their famous red coats

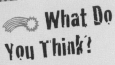
What Do You Think?

What do you think the artist of this image thought about British soldiers? About Patriots?

Boston Massacre

King Street Massacre

On the evening of March 5, 1770, a British **sentry** stood guard in front of the Customs House on King Street in Boston. As he walked his post, a group of local thugs started throwing snowballs. A crowd soon gathered and began tossing chunks of ice.

A squad of soldiers under the command of Thomas Preston arrived to protect the sentry. The crowd grew into a mob armed with sticks and **brickbats**. They encircled Preston and his men. "I hope you do not intend to fire upon the inhabitants," one Bostonian yelled. "By no means, by no means," Preston replied. Suddenly, a shot range out. Then more shots. The smell of gunpowder soaked the air. When the smoke cleared, 11 Boston residents were dead, dying, or wounded. The first to die was Crispus Attucks, a former slave.

No one knew exactly what happened. A silversmith named Paul Revere blamed the massacre on the British. His etching of the incident inflamed public opinion. Thomas Hutchinson, who replaced Bernard as governor of Massachusetts, saw the situation spiraling out of control. He promised swift justice. The soldiers were arrested.

Trial and Repeal

The job of defending the soldiers fell to John Adams, the cousin of Samuel Adams. John Adams disagreed with British policy toward the colonies. Yet, he was a firm believer that laws should be obeyed. With Adams arguing the case, a jury found only two of the soldiers guilty of **manslaughter**.

The shootings were a turning point. Even Britons who wanted a tough American policy admitted that tensions needed to be eased. Britain's new prime minister, Lord Frederick North, changed his position. He had said in 1767 that he would never repeal the taxes. However, after the King Street massacre, North urged for the repeal of the Revenue Act. Parliament agreed. But it refused to revoke the tax on tea. An uneasy calm settled over the colonies for three years. That calm would shatter with the largest "tea party" in history.

🌠 What Do You Know!

By 1770, Africans and African Americans made up nearly 20 percent of the population of the colonies. Almost all of them were slaves. Many fought for America during the Revolutionary War. However, many slaves sided with the British on the promise of gaining their freedom at end of the war.

Many African Americans fought for Great Britain during the Revolutionary War because the British promised freedom from slavery.

Tea in the Harbor

Major Events

1773

May 10
Tea Act passes

December 16
Boston Tea Party

1774

Coercive Acts (Intolerable Acts) passed

March
Boston Harbor closed

September 5
First Continental Congress meets

Tea was the most popular drink in the colonies. When Britain gave the East India Company a virtual **monopoly** on the colonial tea trade, American anger **simmered** until it boiled.

"This Shameful Luxury"

The tax on tea was a leftover from the Townshend Acts. Americans loved to drink tea. Yet, it was a constant reminder that Parliament refused to give up its claim to charge taxes on the colonies. Most Americans refused to buy British tea because of the tax. They purchased less expensive tea smuggled from Holland.

A formal tea service

The British East India Company flag

The British East India Company (EIC) was one of the most powerful institutions in Britain. By 1771, it was near bankruptcy. It had 18 million pounds (over 8 million kg) of **surplus** tea that it could not sell. The company pleaded with Parliament for help.

On May 10, 1773, Parliament passed the Tea Act. Its intent was not to raise revenue. Instead, the law allowed the British East India Company to ship the tea directly to the colonies and sell it at a rock-bottom price. The Americans, however, were still forced to pay the tax.

"
. . . [T]he detested tea for this port . . . is now arrived. . . . [T]he hour of destruction stares you in the face. . . .

—from a handbill published after the HMS *Dartmouth* dropped anchor with a cargo of British tea on November 28, 1773
"

Monopolizing Control

The law benefited the merchants licensed by the East India Company. These merchants were the only ones who could sell tea in the colonies. This undercut the price charged by the merchants who did not have an EIC license. In Boston alone, only five people had an EIC license to sell tea. Three of these people were related to Governor Hutchinson.

Americans realized other British companies could forge a similar monopoly. In Pennsylvania, John Dickinson railed against the Tea Act and the East India Company. "They have levied war," he wrote.

Something had to be done. The clock was ticking. Several tea ships were already en route from England to America in the fall of 1773. Three of those ships—the HMS *Dartmouth,* the HMS *Eleanor,* and the HMS *Beaver*—were bound for Boston.

Disguised Patriots throwing tea overboard from an EIC ship during the Boston Tea Party

Saltwater Tea

Boston had become the most radical colonial town by the time the ships arrived in November 1773. Bostonians assembled at the Old South Meeting House to discuss their options. Samuel Adams urged his fellow citizens to reject British tea, which he called "this shameful luxury." Adams was so persuasive that the crowd voted to return the tea "to the place from whence it came."

On December 16, 1773, a group of men disguised as Mohawk Native Americans slipped aboard each tea ship in Boston Harbor. The "Mohawk warriors" overpowered the crew. They then hurled the chests of tea overboard. "We have only been making a little saltwater tea," one "Mohawk" told his wife upon arriving home that night.

Samuel Adams

People in the War

Samuel Adams

Samuel Adams, a Boston brewer, was instrumental in organizing the Boston Tea Party. He had built a huge following of supporters over the years by mingling in Boston's taverns, lodges, and volunteer fire companies.

Adams was considered by many to be a troublemaker. But he was a shrewd politician, a skilled writer, and a passionate defender for American liberty. He kept the resistance going during a period of calm between 1770 until 1773.

After the Tea Party, Adams traveled to Philadelphia to serve in the Continental Congress. He returned to Massachusetts in 1780 to write the state's first constitution. He later served as its governor (1793–1797).

Joshua Wyeth was just 16 years old when he participated in the Boston Tea Party. Wyeth told a journalist 53 years later what happened that day. His account was published in 1826:

"

The duty on tea gave great umbrage to the colonists generally and in Boston an association was formed in 1770 to drink no tea until the duty was repealed. This course was persisted in 1773 the arrival of 3 ships from England laden with tea caused great disgust. . . . Every effort was made to send these ships back but without success and it was soon evident that the tea would be landed unless some active measures were adopted by the citizens to prevent it.

"A town meeting was called on the afternoon of December 16, 1773 to devise measures for getting rid of this annoyance. . . . Immediately after a detach't [detachment] of about 20 men disguised as Indians . . . marched with silent steps down the isle and so passed by the south door brandishing their tommahaws [tomahawks] in that direction. The appearance of these men created some sensation . . . On leaving the church, they proceeded . . . down Milk Street through . . . to . . . wharves where the tea ships lay.

"Arrived at the wharves they divided into three troops each with a leader gained possession of the ships quietly and proceeded to lighten them of their cargo by hoisting out the boxes and emptying their contents into the dock. No noise was heard except the occasional clink of the hatchet in opening the boxes and the whole business was performed with so much expedition that before 10 o'clock that night the entire cargo of the three vessels were deposited in the docks. . . .

"

Outrage

Parliament had run out of patience, especially with Massachusetts. Many Britons looked on the Americans as traitors. They promised to bring the full weight of the Crown down on their heads. To that end, Lord North drew up a series of regulations called the Coercive Acts. The colonists called them the Intolerable Acts.

The Coercive Acts tried to isolate Massachusetts from the rest of the colonies. The navy closed Boston's port in March 1774, stopping shipments of imported food. In May the British stripped the Massachusetts assembly of its power.

The colonists struck back. The Boston Committee of Correspondence, formed earlier as a way to organize action against Great Britain, organized support in other colonies. They felt the time had come for each colony to meet and find a way to combat the ongoing British assault on American liberty. Representatives from all the colonies, except Georgia, traveled to Philadelphia and formed a Continental Congress. The countdown to armed revolt had begun.

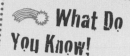

What Do You Know!

A Loyalist was a colonist who supported Britain during the Revolutionary War. Many Loyalists were clergymen, wealthy citizens, and colonial officials. Many fled to Canada, the West Indies, or Britain during the rebellion.

Before long, Patriots burned some buildings in New York in protest against the British.

5

Road to Independence

Major Events

1774

September 5
First Continental Congress meets

October 24
Continental Congress adjourns

1775

April 19
Battles of Lexington and Concord

May
Second Continental Congress meets

July
Congress offers **reconciliation** petition to Britain

August
King George III declares colonies in rebellion

1776

June
Declaration of Independence written

July 2
Declaration of Independence passes

July 4
Declaration of Independence signed

W hen George Washington, Samuel and John Adams, Patrick Henry, and others met in Philadelphia on September 5, 1774, independence was talked about in **hushed** tones. Still, by accepting the Intolerable Acts, the colonists believed they would be giving up their rights as British subjects.

First Continental Congress

British All

The First Continental Congress was called in response to the Intolerable Acts in 1774. The 56 delegates who attended the Continental Congress met in a secret session in Carpenters' Hall in Philadelphia. Up until now, each colony acted independently. They distrusted one another. Some colonies ordered their delegates to seek a solution with Britain. Others were more radical. They wanted to split from Great Britain.

Congressional Agreement

The delegates first agreed to a list of common principles. This included the right to assemble and the right to petition the king. Then they agreed to boycott British goods until Britain lifted the Intolerable Acts. The delegates also said it was against the law for British troops to be in the colonies during a time of peace without the consent of the colonies. Moreover, Americans had a right to life, liberty, their property, and trial by a jury.

Delegates also prepared for war. They urged each colony to put its militia "upon a proper footing," or to be prepared, in case of war. The First Continental Congress adjourned on October 24. Delegates agreed to a Second Continental Congress in May 1775.

John Adams served as a representative to the Continental Congress from Massachusetts. He led the radical group along with his cousin, Samuel Adams.

People in the War
John Adams

John Adams was born on October 30, 1735, and trained as a lawyer. During the Second Continental Congress, he argued that America should be its own country. He also helped write the Declaration of Independence. He became the first vice-president of the United States and the second president after George Washington. He died on July 4, 1826, fifty years after the Declaration of Independence was signed. Thomas Jefferson died the same day.

On the Move

Boston was very unstable during the winter of 1774–1775. Its harbor was closed. Ships rotted at anchor. Commerce was at a standstill. In April Parliament passed the Restraining Act, which prohibited the colonies from trading with any nation other than Britain and the British West Indies. For many Americans, the Restraining Act was the last **humiliation**. The numbers of the Sons of Liberty grew. The British did not worry. To General Thomas Gage and his officers, the colonists were nothing more than "bumpkins" and "illiterate plowboys." Gage's pride ultimately forced him to move against the rebels. He wanted to arrest Samuel Adams and John Hancock. Gage thought they were hiding in Lexington and would soon be in Concord. Concord was also home to a large **cache** of weapons that Gage wanted to capture. The British marched out of Boston on April 18, 1775 towards Concord. The first shots of the American Revolutionary War were fired the next morning.

General Thomas Gage

To Arms

Fighting spread quickly to other colonies. The Second Continental Congress met again in May 1775 at the Pennsylvania State House in Philadelphia. Hancock, along with John Adams, proposed the creation of a Continental Army. Congress selected George Washington as its commander. After arriving in Boston, Washington was not happy with what he saw. His troops were indeed "plowboys" and "bumpkins."

King George III rejected a petition from the Continental Congress for reconciliation. He declared on August 23, 1775 that America was "in an open and avowed Rebellion." The time to turn back had long since passed.

Washington takes command of the Continental Army

Selling Independence

> *Government even in its best state is but a necessary evil; in its worst state an intolerable one.*
>
> —Thomas Paine, from his pamphlet *Common Sense*, 1776

Thomas Paine

By 1776 any thought of mending ties with Great Britain was gone. For John Adams and others, it was time to forge a new nation. Many were skeptical. Breaking ties with Great Britain was beyond radical. Independence needed a salesman. His name was Thomas Paine.

Born in England in 1737, Paine came to America late in 1774. He was 39 years old and a failure at every job he had. Upon his arrival, Paine embraced the idea of independence.

In January 1776 he published a pamphlet called *Common Sense*. In it, Paine argued the case for independence. The "blood of the slain, the weeping voice of nature cries, 'TIS TIME to PART."

Common Sense, the pamphlet published in 1776 by Thomas Paine

Dissolution Debated

Richard Henry Lee of Virginia stood before the Second Continental Congress on June 7, 1776, and made a motion to declare American independence. ". . . [T]hese United Colonies are, and of right ought to be free and independent States . . . ," Lee bellowed.

The delegates debated their **dissolution** from Britain. The radicals said America was ready for independence. Others weren't so sure. Congress postponed a vote until the first week in July. In the meantime, it appointed John Adams, Ben Franklin, Roger Sherman, Robert R. Livingston, and Thomas Jefferson to draw up a declaration by June 28. The task of writing the document fell to Jefferson.

Drafting of the Declaration of Independence

Independence

Thomas Jefferson was a farmer, a slave owner, and a politician. Young and sure of himself, Jefferson was also a thinker who constantly read the writings of great **philosophers**. Their lessons opened new worlds for him.

Jefferson put that knowledge to work when writing the Declaration of Independence. In it, Jefferson listed all the complaints America had with Great Britain and its king. Jefferson argued that governments exist to serve the will of the people, not the other way around. In fact, if people did not like their government, they could change it.

It was a revolutionary concept. Throughout history, people believed whatever rights they enjoyed came from their king or queen. Jefferson now said that people had rights that the government could not take away.

On July 2, Congress unanimously passed the declaration. New York **abstained**. The delegates signed the document on July 4. After Franklin affixed his signature, he said half-jokingly, "We must all hang together, or assuredly we shall all hang separately."

The United States of America was born. A struggle to establish independence lay ahead. But at the end of that struggle, there stood a nation destined to change democracy, and the world, forever.

Jefferson's Declaration

The document Congress signed on July 4, 1776, was not the text Jefferson originally wrote. His first draft was more bold and powerful. In addition to the king and Parliament, Jefferson's original version also blamed the people of Great Britain for the crisis. The people, Jefferson wrote, "have been deaf to the voice of justice."

Before voting, Congress edited Jefferson's original script. It removed most of the criticism of the British people and a long section critical of slavery. In the end, delegates cut 25 percent of the original text.

Signing the Declaration of Independence

GLOSSARY

abstain to not vote, often on principle

ally a nation which agrees to support another, often militarily; the receiving nation will usually agree to aid the supporting nation at a later time of need

American colonies the 13 colonies administered by Great Britain which became the United States; Massachusetts, New Hampshire, Rhode Island, Connecticut, New York, Pennsylvania, New Jersey, Delaware, Maryland, Virginia, North Carolina, South Carolina, Georgia

archaic old, out of use

bedraggled worn and ragged; rough, tired

boycott to refuse to buy, often for a political purpose

brickbat a piece of hard material, often used as a weapon

cache a hiding place for weapons or valuables

colonize to build colonies, or overseas settlements

commodity a good, such as timber or metals, which has value

confiscate to take away; to seize

currency money; especially coins

duties taxes or fees

discontent unhappiness, dissatisfaction

dissent disagreement, usually publically spoken

dissolution breaking up, dissolving

economy the exchange of goods, services, and money

effigy a model or replica of a famous person, often burned

harbor a protected body of water where ships can anchor; often built into a port

hushed quiet, secret

humiliation extreme embarrassment, often causing loss of self-esteem

impose to put upon or force upon

legislature the law-making body, usually made up of representatives of the people

levy to charge or begin a new tax

Loyalist someone who remained loyal to Great Britain; someone who did not want the American colonies to separate from the British Empire

manslaughter the accidental killing of another person

militia a small military unit made up of citizen soldiers

monopoly the economic condition under which a single company has control over the whole market of one good

Parliament the governing body of Great Britain and the United Kingdom; made up of the House of Commons and the House of Lords

Patriot someone who wanted the American colonies to separate from Great Britain

philosopher a thinker who seeks wisdom and knowledge

radical someone whose beliefs and ideas are more extreme than usual

reconciliation coming back together, rebuilding ties

regulars a nickname for British soldiers meaning that they were career or professional soldiers

rescind to take back or cancel

rights the privileges which belong to a citizen

sentry a soldier who stands guard or scouts

simmer a light boil; the stage just before boiling

smuggle to transport illegally, often to avoid taxes

strategy the study of how military force can best be used

surplus extra, more than necessary

surrender to give up or lay down arms

tar and feather to cover someone in hot tar and feathers; a common practice of the Sons of Liberty for their targets

taxes a fee charged by the government on goods or income

tyranny the domination of government or society by a non-democratic individual or group

zeal excited or energetic pursuit of an objective

TIMELINE

1754	*May 28*	French and British clash at Fort Necessity; French and Indian War begins
1759		British troops capture Quebec City
1760		British troops capture Montreal
1763		French and Indian War ends
	May	Pontiac's Rebellion
1764	*April 5*	Sugar Act passes
	September 1	Currency Act passes
1765	*February 17*	Stamp Act passes
	March 24	Quartering Act passes
1767	*June 29*	Townshend Revenue Act (Townshend Acts) passes
1768	*October 1*	British troops occupy Boston
1770	*March 5*	Boston Massacre (King's Street Massacre)
1773	*May 10*	Tea Act passes
	December 16	Boston Tea Party
1774	*September 5*	First Continental Congress meets
	October 24	Continental Congress adjourns
1775	*April 19*	Battles of Lexington and Concord
	May	Second Continental Congress meets
	May 10	Americans capture Fort Ticonderoga
	June 17	British losses near Bunker Hill
	July	Congress offers reconciliation petition to Britain
	July 2	George Washington takes command of the Continental Army
	August	King George III declares colonies in rebellion
1776	*June*	Declaration of Independence written
	July 2	Declaration of Independence passes
	July 4	Declaration of Independence signed

FURTHER READING AND WEBSITES

Books

Aloian, Molly. *George Washington: Hero of the American Revolution*. Crabtree Publishing Company, 2013.

Aloian, Molly. *Phillis Wheatley: Poet of the Revolutionary Era*. Crabtree Publishing Company, 2013.

Clarke, Gordon. *Significant Battles of the American Revolution*. Crabtree Publishing Company, 2013.

Cocca, Lisa Colozza. *Marquis de Lafayette: Fighting for America's Freedom*. Crabtree Publishing Company, 2013.

Mason, Helen. *Life on the Homefront during the American Revolution*. Crabtree Publishing Company, 2013.

Moore, Kay, O'Leary, Daniel. *If You Lived at the Time of the American Revolution*. Scholastic, 1998.

Murphy, Daniel. *The Everything American Revolution Book*. Adams Media, 2008.

Murray, Stuart. *Eyewitness: American Revolution*. Dorling Kindersley Publishing, 2005.

Penner, Lucille Recht. *Liberty! How the Revolutionary War Began*. Random House, 2002.

Perritano, John. *Outcomes of the Revolutionary War*. Crabtree Publishing Company, 2013.

Raum, Elizabeth. *The Revolutionary War: An Interactive History Adventure*. You Choose Books, 2009.

Roberts, Steve. *King George III: The Struggle to Keep America*. Crabtree Publishing Company, 2013.

Websites

http://www.history.com/topics/american-revolution

The History Channel takes an in-depth look at the people, groups, themes, and events that shaped the Revolutionary War.

http://www.historycentral.com/Revolt/causes.html

This website takes readers through the causes of the Revolutionary War.

http://www.bostonmassacre.net/

This site from the Boston Massacre Historical Society gives a clear, concise breakdown of that pivotal moment.

http://www.pbs.org/ktca/liberty/

PBS's look at the American Revolution.

BIBLIOGRAPHY

Books

Davenport, John. *The American Revolution.* Lucent Books, 2007.

Langguth, A.J. *Patriots: The Men Who Started the American Revolution.* Simon & Schuster, 1988.

McCullough, David. *John Adams.* Simon & Schuster, 2001.

McDougall, Walter A. *Freedom Just Around the Corner: A New American History, 1585–1828.* Harper Collins, 2004.

Middlekauff, Robert. *The Glorious Cause: The American Revolution, 1763–1789.* Oxford University Press, 1982.

Miller, John C. and Eric M. Simon. *Origins of the American Revolution.* Little Brown, 1943.

Wood, Gordon S. *Empire of Liberty A History of the Early Republic, 1789-1815 (Oxford History of the United States).* Oxford University Press. 2009.

Websites

"Causes of the American Revolution." *National History Education Clearinghouse.* **http://teachinghistory.org/history-content/beyond-the-textbook/25628**

"Diplomatic Struggles in the Colonial Period: 1750–1775." *U.S. Department of State, Office of the Historian.* **http://history.state.gov/milestones/1750–1775**

Wood, Gordon. "The Intellectual Origins of the American Revolution." **http://spot.colorado.edu/~mcguire/wood.htm**

Index